THE DALAI LAMA

SPIRITUAL LEADER OF THE TIBETAN PEOPLE

P9-DGE-397

JEANNE NAGLE

Britannica®
Educational Publishing

IN ASSOCIATION WITH

ROSEN
EDUCATIONAL SERVICES

Published in 2015 by Britannica Educational Publishing (a trademark of Encyclopædia Britannica, Inc.) in association with The Rosen Publishing Group, Inc.
29 East 21st Street, New York, NY 10010

Distributed exclusively by Rosen Publishing.
To see additional Britannica Educational Publishing titles, go to rosenpublishing.com.

First Edition

<u>Britannica Educational Publishing</u>
J.E. Luebering: Director, Core Reference Group
Anthony L. Green: Editor, Compton's by Britannica

<u>Rosen Publishing</u>
Hope Lourie Killcoyne: Executive Editor
Nelson Sá: Art Director
Nicole Russo: Designer
Cindy Reiman: Photography Manager

Cataloging-in-Publication Data

Nagle, Jeanne, author.
The Dalai Lama: spiritual leader of the Tibetan people/Jeanne Nagle.—First Edition.
    pages cm.—(Making a difference: leaders who changed the world)
Includes bibliographical references and index.
ISBN 978-1-62275-440-3 (library bound)—ISBN 978-1-62275-442-7 (pbk.)—
ISBN 978-1-62275-443-4 (6-pack)
1. Bstan-'dzin-rgya-mtsho, Dalai Lama XIV, 1935—Juvenile literature. I. Title.
BQ7935.B777N35 2014
294.3'923092—dc23
[B]

                                                                    2014001956

Manufactured in the United States of America

Photo Credits:
Cover, p.1 Chris McKay/Getty Images; cover (inset) © Alexander Koerner/Getty Images; pp. 3, 6, 15, 22, 34, 43–45 (background) © iStockphoto.com/yo-ichi; pp. 4–5 Keith Tsuji/Getty Images; pp. 6, 9 Keystone-France/Gamma-Keystone/Getty Images; p. 11 Paula Bronstein/Hulton Archive/Getty Images; p. 12 Manjunath Kiran/AFP/Getty Images; p. 13 Emmanuel Dunand/AFP/Getty Images; p. 15 Jeremy Horner/LightRocket/Getty Images; p. 17 Keystone/Hulton Archive/Getty Images; p. 19 © AP Images; p. 20 Hope Killcoyne; p. 22 Frederic J. Brown/AFP/Getty Images; p. 24 Courtesy George W. Bush Presidential Library and Museum; p. 29 AFP/Getty Images; p. 32 Manan Vatsyayana/AFP/Getty Images; p. 34 Peter Parks/AFP/Getty Images; p. 36 Free Tibet; p. 37 Mark Ralston/AFP/Getty Images; p. 40 Dieter Nagl/AFP/Getty Images; cover and interior graphic elements © iStockphoto.com/BeholdingEye (rays), © iStockphoto.com/JSP007 (interior pages border pattern), Shutterstock.com/abstract (silhouetted figures with map), © iStockphoto.com/traffic analyzer (back cover map).

CONTENTS

INTROD

The Dalai Lama shares Buddhist teachings of peace and nonviolence.

For centuries, the Dalai Lama was the political ruler of Tibet, as well as the leader of the main branch of Tibetan Buddhism. He was also considered the god of compassion who came to Earth to help people.

The followers of Tibetan Buddhism believe in reincarnation, which is the idea that after death a person's soul is born again in a new body. They believe that each Dalai Lama is a rebirth of the first Dalai Lama, who died in 1475. When a Dalai Lama dies, Tibetan Buddhist leaders look for a child born soon thereafter. The child must pass many tests to prove that he is the reincarnated Dalai Lama.

The current Dalai Lama, Tenzin Gyatso, is the fourteenth Dalai Lama. Driven into the mountains of India when China took control of Tibet in 1959, he is no longer a political leader. However, he remains a spiritual leader.

The Dalai Lama travels around the world to promote peace and speak about the Tibetans' desire for political independence. As a Buddhist teacher and promoter of peace and justice, the Dalai Lama is a leader who is making a difference in the lives of many people around the world.

CHAPTER 1

HUMBLE BEGINNINGS, EARLY TROUBLE

Young Lhamo Thondup is pictured here around the time he was declared to be the next Dalai Lama.

Tenzin Gyatso, whose birth name was Lhamo Thondup, was born on July 6, 1935, in the village of Taktser, in the northeastern part of Tibet. His parents were farmers, as were many of the family's neighbors. The family was living in the village of Amdo when a search party arrived, searching for the next Dalai Lama.

QUICK FACT

Tibetan Buddhist leaders use different ways to discover where the Dalai Lama will be reborn. One method is to consult an oracle, who is a holy person believed to get messages from a god. An oracle directed searchers to the region of Amdo.

The young Lhamo Thondup was given several tests, which included choosing special items that had belonged to the thirteenth Dalai Lama. The young boy was identified as the fourteenth Dalai Lama in 1937 and given the spiritual name Tenzin Gyatso.

Tenzin and his family moved to Lhasa, the Tibetan capital. Before his fifth birthday, he was officially given the title of Dalai Lama. He was made a Buddhist monk and moved into Potala Palace, where all Dalai Lamas live, without his family. There, he received a good education, which included spiritual training.

QUICK FACT

When Tenzin was first recognized as the Dalai Lama, a greedy Chinese military leader held him and his family hostage. The Tibetan government paid the ransom, and the family was set free unharmed.

COMING OF AGE QUICKLY

Although Tibet was part of China, it gained a degree of self-government in the early twentieth century. Chinese troops, however, entered Tibet in 1950. In a move to try to keep some independence, the Dalai Lama was named the head of Tibet's government that same year, about five years ahead of schedule. Because he was only fifteen, a regent, or temporary ruler, was given power to rule until the Dalai Lama reached the age of twenty.

The Dalai Lama *(right)* gives China's Mao Tse-tung a scarf during their meeting in the 1950s.

In 1951, China took control of Tibet. Even though he was not an officially recognized government leader anymore, the Dalai Lama stayed in Tibet for seven-and-a-half years, trying to protect the rights of the Tibetan people. He even traveled to China to meet with the country's leader at the time, Mao Tse-tung.

GOING INTO EXILE

As the years went on, the situation in Tibet grew worse. In 1959, Chinese troops killed more than eighty thousand Tibetans who were protesting Chinese rule. The Tibetan people feared for the Dalai Lama's safety and urged him to leave the country. Disguised as a Tibetan soldier, the Dalai Lama escaped from his palace during the night. A small group made up of his family and teachers went with him. They were protected on their journey by Tibetan warriors.

Making their way by riding horses and walking, the group crossed the Himalayan mountains. They were followed by Chinese troops, who had discovered that the Dalai Lama had escaped. On March 13, 1959, the Dalai Lama arrived in India. The Indian government offered the group protection from Chinese forces.

No longer afraid of being captured and returned to Tibet, the Dalai Lama set up his government in an Indian-controlled portion

Women pray in front of Potala Palace, the former home of the Dalai Lama in Tibet.

of the Himalayan mountains. From that day forward he was in exile, which meant he was forced to live in a foreign country in order to stay safe.

QUICK FACTS

The name of the place where the Dalai Lama settled in the Himalayas is Dharamsala. The town was established by the British, who had colonized India until 1947. Being up in the mountains had given the British relief from the summer heat.

Below is a view of Dharamsala, the town where the Tibetan government in exile is based.

A Trusted and Respected Leader

At first the government set up in the Himalayas had no real political power in Tibet, since the Chinese had control of the country. Yet the Dalai Lama was still considered a good leader by the people

Exiles from Tibet sit in a waiting area in Dharamsala.

he had briefly ruled. Tens of thousands of Tibetans followed the Dalai Lama into exile. So many Tibetans came to India to be near the Dalai Lama that the Indian government created special places for them to live, called settlements, across the country.

Although his power as a political figure was greatly weakened while in exile, the Dalai Lama remained a strong spiritual leader. Even though he lived in India, he was still very concerned about keeping the culture and traditions of the Tibetan people alive and well. Toward this end, the Dalai Lama helped convince the Indian government to form the Society of Tibetan Education. This is a separate school system within the Indian school system designed to teach the children of Tibetan refugees about their culture.

CHAPTER 2

Celebrity for a Cause

Being the Dalai Lama is an important position. Obviously, members of the Yellow Hat sect, which is the branch of Tibetan Buddhism that he leads, have known about the Dalai Lama for centuries. So have the people of Tibet, who used to have a government led by him. But outside of Tibet, there were plenty of people who did not know much about the Tibetan spiritual and political leader.

All the Dalai Lamas who came before Tenzin

Monks of the Yellow Hat sect

QUICK FACT

Tibetan Buddhism is not practiced only in Tibet. This form of Buddhism is also popular in Mongolia, Nepal, and Bhutan, as well as parts of India and China.

Gyatso were fairly mysterious. They mainly kept to themselves, living alone in their palace and working mostly in private. Tenzin, however, has made a point of being out in public, traveling and speaking in several countries. He has become the most famous Buddhist teacher in the world. In fact, he is something of a celebrity. And yet, despite his fame and the fuss surrounding his position as a spiritual leader, the Dalai Lama describes himself as a "simple Buddhist monk."

STARTING OUT SLOWLY

The Dalai Lama traveled very little during the early part of his exile. When he did leave his palace in Dharamsala, he would visit his exiled followers in their settlement camps throughout India. Between 1959 and 1966, he made anywhere from one to seven visits to different Indian cities in a year. He visited the large city of Delhi quite frequently.

Even though he mostly stayed put within India during this time, the Dalai Lama still had contact with the outside world. In fact, early in his exile, on June 20, 1959, he held a press conference to officially reject the forced agreement that led to China's taking over

Greeted by officials, the Dalai Lama *(center)* arrives in India in 1959.

control of Tibet. This agreement was known as the Seventeen-Point Agreement.

On the first anniversary of his escape to India, the Dalai Lama spoke out against China again. First, he made a public announcement encouraging the Tibetan people who were in exile to keep their culture alive. As stated in his website, www.dalailama.com, he also said that Tibetans would eventually regain their freedom "with truth, justice and courage as our weapons..."

REACHING OUT THROUGH WRITING

Another way the Dalai Lama communicated with people was to write books. The first

FRIENDING HIS HOLINESS

In addition to writing books and making speeches, the Dalai Lama has become popular online, through the Internet and social networking. As of April 2014, his Facebook account had more than eight million "likes."

book he wrote, an autobiography titled *My Land and My People*, was published in 1962. Four years later, *The Opening of the Wisdom-Eye* was on store bookshelves. This book was an introduction to Buddhism.

In total, the Dalai Lama has written more than one hundred books. Most are about how Buddhist beliefs and practices can help people live a good and happy life. Several have been best sellers. The popularity of his books has also

His Holiness, who is also a popular author, signs his books at a 2010 event in Slovenia.

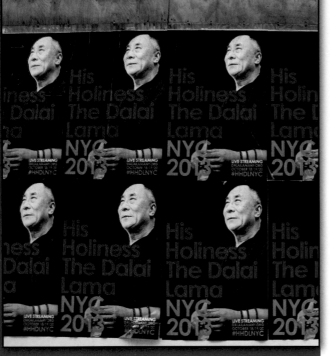

Posters announce an appearance by the Dalai Lama in New York City.

helped make the Dalai Lama a celebrity.

HITTING THE ROAD

Later on, the Dalai Lama traveled quite a bit outside of India. He made his first trip outside of his new home country in 1967, when he visited Japan and Thailand. He then traveled to several European countries in 1973, and he went to the United States and Canada for the first time in 1979. During his travels, he spoke at colleges and universities. He also met with political and religious leaders. As of January 2014, he had traveled to more than sixty-seven countries, visiting six of the world's seven continents.

QUICK FACT

Followers of the Dalai Lama also became world travelers. They wound up establishing schools and monasteries, which are where monks live and worship, in Europe, North America, and Australia.

MESSAGES TO THE WORLD

The Dalai Lama has long dedicated his life to two main goals. One of these goals is to share his faith. He reaches this goal through his speeches and books, which discuss the main ideas and practices of Buddhism. Sometimes he explains Buddhist scriptures, or sacred writings. He also notes how people of different religions can work together toward peace.

His second goal has been to make sure the world knows about Tibet's troubles with China. He has become famous for speaking out about the lack of freedom in his home country.

CHAPTER 3

Notable Works and Achievements

The Dalai Lama certainly does not seek attention or recognition. Yet for years he has received praise and awards for his good works. He has been applauded by many nations, including the United States and Canada, for moving his government in exile closer to democracy. He created the Dalai Lama Trust, an organization aimed at keeping Tibetan culture strong

Actor Richard Gere *(right)* is one of the Dalai Lama's biggest supporters in the United States.

among the exiled masses and sharing parts of that culture with the rest of the world. Finally, his tireless work toward peace and understanding has gained the attention and admiration of people everywhere.

A MOVE TOWARD DEMOCRACY

When he was the political leader of Tibet, the Dalai Lama was considered a cross between a king and a god. At first, he held the same kind of power in exile. But because he believed very strongly that Tibetans should have certain freedoms, he led a push to make his government in India a democracy.

In 1963, the Dalai Lama wrote a constitution, or set of laws, that he wanted to use once Tibetans gained control of their own country again. Democracies use constitutions to let people have a say in how they are governed and to guarantee them certain freedoms. The Dalai Lama's constitution stressed the freedoms of speech and religion, as well as the right to gather together in public for just about any reason. These are the same types of rights granted under

An early handwritten copy of the Tibetan constitution

the United States Constitution.

The constitution was written to be used when Tibet was its own free nation again. For years, the government in exile operated by informally following the guidelines of the constitution meant for a free and independent Tibet. Then, in 1991, a separate set of official rules for the Tibetan government based in India was created. This was known as the Charter of the Tibetans-in-Exile, or the Tibetan Charter. The charter was created by members of the Commission of

QUICK FACT

The Dalai Lama does not want democratic freedom only for the people of Tibet. He has supported pro-democracy movements elsewhere, including China.

Tibetan People's Deputies, who are elected representatives of Tibetan exiles.

The Dalai Lama officially approved the charter on June 28, 1991. This was yet another step by the Dalai Lama to bring democracy to Tibet.

FIVE POINTS FOR PEACE

Throughout the 1960s and 1970s, repeated attempts to gain independence for Tibet failed. But that didn't stop the Dalai Lama from trying to solve the problems of his people and give them back their freedoms. In 1987, in front of

QUICK FACT

Tibetans took another step toward democracy in 2011, when elections were held for the position of prime minister of the exiled government. Up until then, a high-level monk had been acting as prime minister without being elected by the people.

members of the United States Congress, he spoke about a new plan for Tibet called Five Points for Peace.

The five points stated that:

1. Tibet should be turned into a zone of "peace and nonviolence."
2. China should stop sending Chinese settlers to live in Tibet and leave the area to the Tibetan people.
3. All nations should respect the human rights and democratic freedoms of the Tibetan people.

4. The natural environment should be restored, and China should stop dumping nuclear waste in Tibet.

5. China should seriously enter into negotiations regarding the future of Tibet and relations between the two countries.

A PLAN TO TAKE THE "MIDDLE WAY"

The fifth point in the Five Point Plan required that China negotiate with the exiled Tibetan government to find a solution that gave something to both parties. Since China was not willing to negotiate or give up control, the Dalai Lama came up with a compromise plan to regain some Tibetan freedoms. He wanted to find a "middle way approach" between complete independence for Tibet and the country's total absorption into the People's Republic of China.

During a 1988 session of the European Parliament in the French city of Strasbourg, the Dalai Lama proposed that Tibet have its own government but work with China to handle national and foreign affairs. This became known as the Strasbourg Accord.

NEITHER TOO MUCH NOR TOO LITTLE

In Buddhist teachings, "the middle way" is the path that lies between living a selfish life of luxury and denying oneself even simple pleasures. The idea is said to have come directly from the Buddha himself.

Because they had control of Tibet, the Chinese did not want to negotiate at all. The "middle way" plan of the Strasbourg Accord was rejected by the Chinese government.

NOBEL PRIZE WINNER

Although his compromise plan did not bring about a free and independent Tibet, the

His Holiness greets members of the media after winning the Nobel Prize.

Dalai Lama did get high praise for trying to peacefully achieve his goal. In 1989, he was awarded the Nobel Peace Prize, largely because of his Five Points Plan and the Strasbourg Accord. The Dalai Lama was very humble during his acceptance speech, declaring that "I am no one special."

With money received from winning the Nobel Peace Prize, he established the Foundation for Universal Responsibility. The foundation tries to find common ground between people of various faiths and seeks nonviolent ways to protect basic human rights and freedoms.

QUICK FACT

The Dalai Lama Foundation was created by friends and students of the Dalai Lama in 2002. The foundation's programs center mainly on the study of peace and nonviolence.

The Dalai Lama Trust

In 2009, the Dalai Lama set up a trust, or a pool of money set aside for a specific purpose. The Dalai Lama Trust is meant to support causes the Dalai Lama has worked toward most of his life. These include education, saving the environment, working toward peace, making connections between faith and science, and the protection of Tibetan culture.

The Dalai Lama Trust is run by a board of trustees. The Dalai Lama is the chairman of the board. Money in the trust is given to

Quick Fact

In 2007, the Dalai Lama received the United States Congressional Gold Medal. The award is given to those who have made a lasting achievement in their field. It is the highest nonmilitary honor that the U.S. Congress can give.

individuals and groups in the form of grants and scholarships.

THE TEMPLETON PRIZE

In 2012, the Dalai Lama was given another important honor. The Templeton Prize is given to a living person who is an exceptional leader in spiritual matters. As he had when

A young Indian girl studies at a school run by Save the Children, a charity that received most of the Dalai Lama's Templeton Prize money.

he accepted the Nobel Peace Prize, the Dalai Lama played down his importance in winning the award. He took the spotlight off of himself and placed it on matters of faith and peace.

Also, as when he had won the Nobel Prize, he put the prize money attached to the honor to good use. Most of the (approximately) $1.8 million was donated to the charity group Save the Children in India. Save the Children is an international children's rights organization that also gives aid to children and families during wars and natural disasters.

The rest of the prize money was given to the Mind and Life Institute, which supports research into the connection between science and spirituality. Some money also went to a fund that pays for Tibetan monks to earn science degrees.

CHAPTER 4

WHAT THE FUTURE MAY HOLD

The Dalai Lama has said many times that he is merely a simple man and a humble monk. Spiritually speaking, however, he is thought to be a god on Earth. Of course, even if he is a bit god-like, he does not have the power to predict the future. The only thing that seems sure in the future for the Dalai Lama is that he will continue to teach others about Buddhism and fight for the rights of the Tibetan people.

A young Tibetan monk stays warm while attending an event in China.

Out of Sight, but not Out of Mind

The Dalai Lama has been in exile for most of his time as the top Tibetan leader. In all that time, he has never stopped working for, and speaking out about, the troubles facing his people and country. Because of that, he has stayed a respected and beloved leader— even among Tibetans who still live in the Chinese-controlled territory.

The popularity of the Dalai Lama in Tibet has upset the Chinese government. Officials in China have tried their best to take away the Dalai Lama's popularity in his homeland. Keeping him out of the country and out of power wasn't enough. To squash his popularity, they decided they would have to somehow silence him.

In 2013, the Chinese government took extra steps to keep any reminders of the Dalai Lama out of Tibet. People were already punished for having pictures of the Dalai Lama in their homes, as well as for listening to or reading the text of speeches he has made. New steps included taking away illegal satellite dishes so

QUICK FACT

According to Free Tibet's website, between March 2011 and January 2014, more than 120 people have set themselves on fire to protest Chinese control of Tibet. This is an extreme form of protest that has both political and religious significance in Tibet.

The Free Tibet website (http://www.freetibet.org) provides information on Tibet and the fight to free the region from Chinese rule.

that people could not receive televised news of the Dalai Lama and keeping an even closer watch on how people used the Internet.

PUSHING BACK

The extra push to keep the Dalai Lama and his messages out of Tibetan minds has been met with anger and some public protests in Tibet.

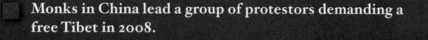

Monks in China lead a group of protestors demanding a free Tibet in 2008.

37

Buddhist monks in particular have shown their strong dislike for the policies of the Chinese government. Among the protestors' demands has been the return of the Dalai Lama to Tibet so that he could resume leadership of the country.

In 2008, the Dalai Lama spoke about being very sad that injuries and deaths, on both the Tibetan and Chinese sides, had occurred during major protests across Tibet that year. He also reminded Tibetans everywhere that they should practice nonviolence at all times, regardless of the situation.

GIVING UP POLITICAL CONTROL

Something happened in 2011 that had many questioning what the role of the Dalai Lama would be in years to come. That year, during a speech he gives every year on the anniversary of his leaving Tibet, Tenzin Gyatso announced that he would no longer act as the political leader of the Tibetan government in exile. In other words, he was resigning from the nonreligious part of his job.

This decision was made mainly because the Dalai Lama felt that the government of Tibet should be more democratic—a long-held wish of his. Putting officials elected by the Tibetan people in charge made more sense for a democracy.

On May 29, 2011, the Dalai Lama officially signed over his political power to an elected prime minister. He has kept his position as the spiritual leader of Tibet.

SEARCHING FOR THE FIFTEENTH DALAI LAMA

Another discussion about the future concerned who would be the next Dalai Lama and where he would be found. The Chinese government had stated that the next reincarnation of the Dalai Lama would come from inside Tibet. Many people believed this was an attempt by China to control who the next Tibetan spiritual leader would be. The Chinese would, of course, prefer to have a Buddhist leader who did not challenge their political authority. If the next Dalai Lama came from inside Tibet, they could better

The Dalai Lama greets children at Vienna's SOS Children's Village, a space for orphans and other kids in need.

control what he said and did, since he would be under their rule.

The current Dalai Lama, however, has told his people that he believes the next Dalai Lama will be a Tibetan in exile. As he said in a 2004 interview with *Time* magazine, "My life

QUICK FACT

On the fiftieth anniversary of Dr. Martin Luther King Jr.'s "I Have a Dream" speech, the Dalai Lama revealed a similar hope for the future. In a speech on August 28, 2013, he said, "I always have one dream that within this century the world truly becomes a real happy human family."

is outside Tibet, therefore my reincarnation will logically be found outside." Such a thing would make more sense to the people of Tibet. A Dalai Lama born in exile would be much more likely to want what they want—a free and democratic Tibet—than one living under Chinese control.

REBORN OR NOT?

There is some question, brought up by Tenzin Gyatso himself, as to whether or not the idea of the Dalai Lama being reincarnated should continue after he dies. Mostly he is concerned that reincarnation will be used as a political tool, rather than as the spiritual belief that it was always meant to be.

As a fan of the democratic process, he has said that he will wait until he turns ninety and let the Tibetan people decide if there should be a fifteenth reincarnation. Until then, the Dalai Lama remains a strong leader, fighting for his people and their spiritual beliefs.

TIMELINE OF ACHIEVEMENTS

Dec. 17, 1933: The thirteenth Dalai Lama, Thubten Gyatso, dies.

July 6, 1935: Lhamo Thondup is born.

1937: Lhamo Thondup is identified as the fourteenth Dalai Lama and given the spiritual name Tenzin Gyatso.

1939: Tenzin is publicly declared the fourteenth Dalai Lama.

1940: Enthroned as the Dalai Lama; begins his education as a Buddhist monk.

1942: Takes vows as a monk.

1950: Becomes the ruler of Tibet.

1951: China took control of Tibet.

July 1954–June 1955: Meets with Chinese leader Mao Tse-tung and other leaders for peace talks.

1959: Tenzin escapes to India.

1963: Presents a draft democratic constitution for Tibet.

1967: First visit abroad, to Japan and Thailand, since going into exile.

1973: First visit to the West.

1987: Presents Five Point Plan.

1988: Delivers "middle-way" plan in Strasbourg, France.

1989: Awarded the Nobel Peace Prize.

1991: Furthers democratic reforms by overseeing and enforcing the Charter of the Tibetans-in-Exile.

1992: Begins democratic elections of Tibetan assembly deputies.

2007: Receives the U.S. Congressional Gold Medal.

2011: Formally resigns as the political leader of Tibet.

2012: Honored with the Tempelton Prize.

- **Kofi Annnan.** As secretary-general of the United Nations from 1997 to 2006, Kofi Annan led the UN through a period of outstanding productivity and reform. Annan and the United Nations won the Nobel Peace Prize in 2001.

- **Aung San Suu Kyi.** Following in the footsteps of her father, Aung San Suu Kyi has become a leader in the fight for human rights and democratic freedoms in Myanmar (formerly Burma).

- **Bill and Hillary Clinton.** Known for their public service in the United States government, the Clintons are also philanthropic, or charitable, leaders. They founded the Clinton Foundation in 2001.

- **Bill and Melinda Gates.** The Microsoft founder and his wife have given millions to worthy causes, making them leaders in business and charitable giving.

- **Pope Francis.** As the head of the Roman Catholic Church, Pope Francis has led by example. By living simply and showing compassion and acceptance, he has helped change the image of the church for the better.

• **Sonia Sotomayor.** Sonia Sotomayor's leadership skills are on display in her position as a Supreme Court justice. As one of the major decision makers who can change the course of U.S. history, she also serves as a role model for Hispanic women.

compassion The feeling of wanting to help someone who is in trouble or needs help.

culture The collected beliefs and customs of a group of people.

democratic Based on a form of government in which the people choose leaders by voting.

exile The state of being forced to leave one's country or home.

humble The belief that one is no better than any other person.

monastery A place where monks live and work together.

oracle A person through whom a god is believed to speak.

predict To say what is going to happen in the future.

promote To help make something happen or increase.

refugee A person who flees for safety, especially to a foreign country.

regent A person who rules a kingdom when the king or queen is unable to rule.

reincarnation The belief that the soul experiences rebirth in a new body.

resign To officially or formally give up a job or other position.

sect A religious body within a larger group, consisting of members having similar beliefs. One such example is the Yellow Hat sect (or order) of Tibetan Buddhism, which is led by the Dalai Lama.

spiritual Having to do with religious or otherwise deeply held personal beliefs.

BOOKS

Ananthraman, Aravinda. *The 14th Dalai Lama: Buddha of Compassion*. London, England: Puffin Books, 2011.

Eckel, Malcolm David. *Buddhism*. New York, NY: Rosen Publishing, 2010.

Harris, Joseph. *Tibet* (Global Hotspots). Salt Lake City, UT: Benchmark Books, 2010.

Kimmel, Elizabeth Cody. *Boy on the Lion Throne: The Childhood of the 14th Dalai Lama*. New York, NY: Flash Point (Roaring Book Press), 2009.

Sullivan, Ann Marie, and Jiang-Jiang Chen. *Dalai Lama: Spiriual Leader of Tibet*. Broomall, PA: Mason Crest, 2013.

WEBSITES

Because of the changing nature of Internet links, Rosen Educational Services has developed an online list of websites related to the subject of this book. This site is updated regularly. Please use this link to access the list:

http://www.rosenlinks.com/mad/dalai